Toxic Love

The Illusion of Self-Worth

Toxic Love

The Illusion of Self-Worth

by

Malcolm Smith

PILLAR
BOOKS & PUBLISHING
COMPANY

P. O. Box 471692
Tulsa, Oklahoma 74147-1692

Toxic Love
The Illusion of Self-Worth
ISBN 1-880089-12-2
Copyright © 1992 by Malcolm Smith
Malcolm Smith Ministries
P. O. Box 29747
San Antonio, Texas 78229

Published by:
Pillar Books & Publishing Co.
P. O. Box 471692
Tulsa, Oklahoma 74147-1692
United States of America

Cover design: DB & Associates

Book production: sigma graphics, ltd.

Editor: Elizabeth Sherman

Table of Contents

Toxic Love

The Illusion of Self-Worth

Chapter One

MARTYRDOM

WITHOUT PURPOSE

Are you exhausted by the demands people make on you? Are you a person other people suck dry? Do you answer their every call and then feel weak and used? Or do you ignore them and then condemn yourself because you feel you should have been there for them? Do you go through life trying to be everything to everybody, or feeling ashamed or angry that they have discovered you to be weak and unable to help?

Does someone else call the shots in your life...a husband, wife, teenage child, or perhaps a mother who has not yet let you leave the nest, though you have a family of your own? Does that someone else control whether you feel happy or sad, whether you feel good about yourself or whether you feel life is not worth living?

And the most important question of all is, do you believe that by letting others control and drain you, you are loving them and being to them what God wants you to be? Do you feel you are living a self-less life and will soon be rewarded by a change in the other person or persons which will bring about the happiness you long for?

If you find yourself answering "yes" to any of these questions, then it is possible you have fallen for one of the most despicable lies of the devil—a lie that will keep you from enjoying all that Christ has purchased for you. It will, in fact, leave you in a state of misery and despair much of the time.

True Love's Counterfeit

Jesus described the one all-encompassing mark of a believer when He said, **By this all men will know that you are My disciples, if you have love for one another** (John 13:35).

This love is not a vague, soft "niceness" that believers show to one another. He defined the kind of love He was talking about in the same passage. We are to love one another**...even as I have loved you** (John 13:34). The same love that was first seen in Jesus Christ is now lived out and demonstrated in us by the supernatural power of the Holy Spirit.

However, before we can understand how His kind of love can literally be seen in us, we must look at the biggest hindrance to His love working through us, which is what I call "toxic love." Toxic love is a false, counterfeit love that is passed off as the real thing in today's world. It is a toxic, poisonous love because it originates in what the Bible calls "the flesh," which is completely selfish and self-centered.

Paul made an interesting, though passing, reference to counterfeit love in his great exegesis of love, First Corinthians 13. Verse 3 says, **...and if I deliver my body to be burned, but do not have love, it profits me nothing.** He said that a person may go so far as to give their body as a martyr to be burned, but if they did not have love, their ultimate sacrifice of life itself would be for nothing. In fact, in verse 1, he speaks of Christianity expressed without love as **a noisy gong or clanging cymbal.** Instead of being an expression of Christ, this pseudo act of service would be a hollow noise, jarring to the Spirit.

Paul is speaking of motive, the *source* of a person's actions rather than the action itself. An action can look right, in itself, but if it is coming from the wrong source, it can exhaust us, reducing us to a heap of ashes. To the recipients of the action, it will be nothing but a hollow, empty sound. Paul

3

makes it clear that unless the act of handing over our bodies for sacrifice has its source in the love of God, it amounts to zero.

But what could cause us to offer ourselves as martyrs for no reason? Why would we let ourselves be reduced to a heap of ashes if it accomplished nothing? For someone to go to such lengths, they must believe that what they are doing gives meaning to their life—that it gives them their very identity as a human being. To find such meaning and significance is man's greatest quest.

Created to be Loved

When God created man, He placed within him certain needs that He alone could fill. Knowing the Creator in a love union distinguishes the human from all other creatures; here he finds the reason for his existence and his identity as a person. God's bestowed love is the fuel for every man; severed from that love, he cannot function as the person God created him to be. The need for love could only be met by a relationship with the God Who Himself is love and the source of love in all His creation. Man's destiny in creation was, and still is, to live in union with Love Himself.

Man's sense of significance and worth did not come from contemplating himself, but only as he looked to his origin and source, his Creator. *His*

*self-worth was bestowed upon him in God's uncon-
ditional love for him, a state of being which he
enjoyed—unearned and undeserved—simply
because he was alive and breathing.*

The Lie

Into the garden paradise, the devil came and
enticed man with the Lie that was to shape the rest
of human history. The Lie, simply stated, said that to
live in union with God, receiving and revealing His
love in dependent faith and obedience, was not the
only option open to mankind.

Satan offered an alternative meaning to man's
existence, one that promised to shatter the myth that
he was a mere dependent creature and bring him to
his fullest potential of being a god, independent of his
Creator. To enter this life of total fulfillment
demanded that he declare himself independent of the
Creator, at which point he would discover vast
resources of wisdom, power, and ability to live his life.

Man believed the Lie and, in declaring his inde-
pendence, severed himself from God. No longer in
vital *union* with Him, but *alongside* of Him,
he acknowledged that God existed, but remained
quite independent of Him. In this condition, man
lost his consciousness of being loved and, therefore,
the source of his significance and value within the
creation.

Since the Fall in the Garden of Eden, man has believed the Lie, which is that in and of himself, he can be perfect, self-contained, self-sufficient, and totally in control of his destiny. He has reached for the goal of being superman, with a life that has meaning, joy, peace, and power—all independent of God. He tenaciously believes that one day he will achieve it all, and God will even let him into His heaven saying, "You did a good job without Me!"

But man soon comes to the sickening realization that, however stubbornly he believes the Lie, he is unable to make it work in his life. He does not have a life with meaning, joy, peace, and power. Instead, he suffers from the real guilt of sin and the lost consciousness of love and self-worth. Finally, there is shame, brought about by the knowledge that he cannot be the independent superman the devil promised he could be.

Where does he now turn for love and the sense of self-worth he knows he was made for? He turns to his fellow human beings. He looks to other creatures to give him the assurance that he is lovable, significant, important, and valuable.

Understand the path he has chosen. It is doomed to failure from the start! *If love originates in God alone, another creature cannot give man what his heart is craving. But worse, in choosing this path, man has placed a creature in the place reserved for God. He is an idolater with idols made of flesh, vainly believing that the idols will bring the answer to the emptiness within.*

Paul spoke of this in Romans 1:25 when he described the downward spiral of the human race: **For they exchanged the truth of God for a lie, and worshiped and served the creature rather than the Creator....**

Please—Please Me!

One way this is seen in our everyday lives, yet not recognized as the idolatry it is, is in our relationships with the people around us—especially those in need—who demand our time, and suck and drain us dry with their needs. We want to help, to make everything in their lives right. We want to make them happy. You might say, we want to be their savior, meeting all their needs.

When we have achieved our goal of making them happy, and they give their smile of approval, their murmur of praise, we feel lovable. The warm glow of "feeling good about ourselves" flushes through our being. We feel important, significant as a person. Everything is, and forever will be wonderful.

Strangely, the person we live to make happy is often the source of all our hurts and pain! A wife beater, an alcoholic, a drug user, the teenage delinquent, the workaholic who abuses by neglect...the list goes on and on. The craving to make them happy, to save them from all their problems, and to make everything right becomes the meaning of our lives. The mirage of a day when everything will be perfect draws the captive onward to keep meeting needs.

This person for whom we martyr ourselves doesn't have to be an addict or an emotionally dependent person—this toxic love spills into all of our relationships. We go through life seeking the happiness of everyone else in return for the elusive feeling of self-worth and the sense of being loved, which we may fleetingly experience from time to time.

Of course, most of the time, we fail to be everything the other person wants us to be, and failure plunges us into oceans of guilt and shame. Feelings of worthlessness and rejection flood us when we have failed to please the other person. Many people live in this kind of guilt most of the time.

The Toxic Lover

Why do such people keep going back for more, even though they come away saying, "I will never do that again. I am going to mind my own business. No one appreciates me"? It is because their identity as a person depends on being affirmed and made to feel good by the needy taker. *What they were created to receive only from God, they are searching for in the creature.* To give it up would be to give up their perception of their personhood.

This need for affirmation is born of the same lie that spawned the false gospel that says we must perform to be lovable to God. We are not loving from the inner fullness of knowing God loves us, unconditionally and without limits—a loving which springs from His bestowed sense of worth. Ours is a toxic, false love that is born out of man's separation from God's love. It is a manipulative performance, intended to be a human substitute for the love from God that has been rejected. Exchanging God's unconditional love for this poisonous substitute ultimately destroys both the toxic lover and the needy taker.

The toxic lover has fantasies of being savior and messiah to the needy in their family, at the office, and among their friends. In fact, they feel responsible for making the whole world happy! This is the person who always comes through for the family, and the family always knows to whom they can turn. The reward they receive is those warm words, "We knew we could count on you!" They feel important and significant, because another person needs them. They feed on the need to be needed.

Upside-Down Responsibilities

When the savior fails to save, and the messiah fails to provide all that is needed, the guilt is devastating. They have failed and, in their minds, that is equated with being a failure in their essential selves. The possibility of that happening sends many of these people into a paralysis of fear. They refuse to get involved, for they know they will not be able to meet all of the needs. These people live in guilt for what they ought to be doing; they berate themselves as worthless and useless.

This counterfeit love leaves us stumbling in darkness in our relationships. It creates a muddled reversal of responsibilities. Someone who expects to receive their sense of worth, love, and acceptance from another human's response lives by the moods of those they seek to help. They see every emotion of that other person as *their* responsibility.

If the person from whom they so desire to gain affirmation, love, and acceptance is angry today, immediately the thought springs to mind, "What have I done? If they are angry, it must be my fault!" If they sit in sulky silence, guilt floods the toxic lover: "I must have done something to upset them!" Of course, the opposite is also true. When they are happy, counterfeit love is exultant, "I must have done something to make them happy today! See, I am a good person!"

This reversal of responsibilities works another way, too. If I am angry, I do not see that I am responsible for my emotions. I blame the other person for their failure to respond to me as I wanted them to and believe they should. If I am sad, it is because the other person will not change. My happiness or sadness is as changeable as the weather, depending on the other person's approval or disapproval of my actions.

This is totally against Scripture, which teaches throughout that we each are responsible for our own emotions and actions. Others are responsible for what they do and for their moods; I am responsible for mine. Even if you do wrong to me, I am responsible for my anger and bitterness. I cannot blame you.

Toxic love reverses all responsibilities, turns life into a living hell, and calls the resulting upside-down world "normal"!

Chapter Two

COUNTERFEIT

CHRISTIAN SERVICE

The heart of toxic love's deception is found in the fact that much of the behavior we just described sounds so much like Christian love. In congregations of all denominations, one can find pastors who operate from this mindset, along with those who hold positions of key leadership. Tragically, works that are a product of toxic love are portrayed in many churches as being humble, wrought by selfless servants of the church. But toxic love is the counterfeit of humility and service.

Larry

I remember Larry, who poured out his heart to me while I was visiting his mission station in West Africa. When we talked about his understanding of serving God and why he was in Africa at all, his problem became obvious. He had little or no concept of a God who loved him simply because he was alive. He sincerely believed he had to do something great and keep up the performance in order to be worthy of God's love.

He told me of the missionary meeting in Texas, where he answered the appeal to volunteer as a missionary. The speaker that night passionately outlined the great need and the few workers, if any, to fill the opportunities. He ended by asking, "If you don't go, who will?" Larry decided to volunteer and walked forward to the front of the church along with a handful of others. Through the prayer which followed, and the closing words of the speaker, he felt that his decision had earned him a place in God's elite.

He had lived on this feeling until after he had been in Africa a few months. At that time, the heat, the living conditions, the infighting among the other missionaries, and the fact that he had not even begun to achieve the goals he had set while in preparation in the States finally got to him. He was a mental, emotional, and spiritual wreck; he fell into despair, feeling he had failed God and the people.

When he came to talk to me, he hated the country he was in, despised both the people he worked with and those to whom he was supposed to be ministering, and wondered if he had ever known God!

Joan

There is always at least one in a church upon whom the pastor knows he can depend, someone who will come through in every need and crisis. Joan was one of these "beyond-the-call-of-duty" believers. She could never say no, even though, as she was saying yes, she knew she must be out of her mind! She was spread so thin helping others, that she had no time for the nurturing of her own spiritual life.

Joan rarely took a vacation and, when questioned, she would actually feel guilty at the thought of resting on a beach, when there was so much to be done at home and in the church. She gave her happy little smile, "After all, if I don't do it, who will?"

After a job well done, she would beam, standing in the pastor's office as she received the accolade that would keep her happy for days to come: "I knew we could depend on you, Joan!" But if they forgot to thank her, or if her act of service was omitted from the bulletin, she would sit at home and cry inside, "No one cares about me! I slave day and night and never a mention or thank you!"

Joan is a very lonely lady who is seeking to be loved and accepted through serving others. She has such a need for that love, that she cannot say no to any opportunity.

Other Martyrs

There is the mother who believes she must be involved in the marriages of her children, including their finances and the raising of her grandchildren. She worries and frets over every part of their lives, and when she is unable to help, she has insomnia, feeling she has failed them and is a failure as a mother.

That dear lady, and many variations of her, is giving a twist to the ancient Lie that man first believed in the Garden of Eden. She believes she is God in other people's lives! She could put a plaque over her door, "Our Lady of Perpetual Responsibility"!

This woman believes that she should be omnipresent, omniscient, and omnipotent, so as to be able to solve everyone's problems. And she never lacks for people with problems! In this fallen world, there are plenty of people with real needs, and many more who are working out their sinfulness by wanting others to be responsible for them, to make them the center of attention, and to enable them to continue their sinful habits.

Finally, there is always the spouse of an alcoholic or drug addict, who believes they are loving the person by protecting them with lies, covering for them, and making excuses for them with their employer. True love would support the problem person, while making them face the devastating results of the choices they have made.

The Boomerang Intention

What all of these people call love, or even service to God, is not the God kind of love that Jesus said was the mark of the believer. In fact, it is not love at all, but a subtle selfishness, the reverse of the love Jesus came to birth in us! It is a toxic substitute for real love. This false love reaches out to others so that it may momentarily know the fleeting feeling of being loved and accepted in return by the person and by God. Like the aborigine, this person sends out their boomerang of service in order to have it return to them with the love and acceptance they seek.

Of the God kind of love the Scripture says, **...perfect love casts out fear...**(First John 4:18). Toxic love is governed by the uneasy fear of not being what one should be for God. Moreover, it is shot through with the everpresent fear of failing to be enough for the person or persons it seeks to care for, save, or make happy. If the toxic lover fails to help the person in need, then they are attended by feelings of guilt, shame, and worthlessness.

All of these people burn out, dying inside through their attempts to help, save, and play messiah in the lives of others. The tragedy is that most of them believe they have made the martyr's sacrifice and have a great reward waiting, when all they have is a heap of ashes!

The Character of Toxic Love

This false and toxic love must fail, for it has its origin in man's sinful desire to find a substitute for the love of God in his fellow creatures. God's love, revealed in Jesus Christ, is carefully defined:

Love is patient, love is kind. It does not envy, it does not boast, it is not proud. It is not rude, it is not self-seeking, it is not easily angered, it keeps no record of wrongs. Love does not delight in evil but rejoices with the truth. It always protects, always trusts, always hopes, always perseveres. Love never fails....
First Corinthians 13:4-8a (NIV)

Toxic love is the reverse of this love. This counterfeit love can be very impatient and even unkind to the person who does not respond to its manipulations; it shows itself as jealousy if it perceives that another is capturing the praise it seeks. It is given to bragging on its accomplishments, comparing itself with others who are not as dedicated. It is capable of rudeness in order to get its own way.

Above all, it seeks its own, and if it does not achieve its intended results, it can become irritable, angry, and bitter, remembering, sometimes for years, the wrongs done against it. This false love does not want to face the truth about the person or persons it is seeking to rescue, but rather denies the real problem. It will always fail and is in a perpetual state of falling into despair, shame, and the sense of being a total failure.

Chapter Three

OUR LIVING BLUEPRINT

Jesus said that we are to love one another *as He has loved us,* and that this would be proof that we are His disciples (John 13:34,35). In so saying, He made Himself the norm for the love He spoke about. If we are going to understand what love really is, we shall find it first defined and demonstrated in the person and life of the Lord Jesus.

Jesus Christ is God with us, the God Who took to Himself our humanity and became a true member of His own creation. We are looking at the person Who was 100 percent God, but Who lived among us an authentic human life as 100 percent man. *Christians often forget that Jesus demonstrated the kind of life that mankind was originally created to live; He is the living blueprint of what normal man should be like.*

Life With Abba

At the heart of this normal man's life is His relationship to God, His Father. Man was created a spirit being, which means that he relates *primarily* to God and not to the physical world. As human beings, our mental, emotional, and, more times than we realize, our physical health spring out of our spirit center where we know and are known by God. At that center, Jesus lived in the fullest consciousness of His Father's love.

The words Jesus spoke at age twelve, recorded in Luke 2:49, indicate to us that He already had a highly developed sense of God's love for Him. In His native Hebrew language, He called God His Abba, which is baby talk, the first word Hebrew parents expected their baby to say. The nearest English equivalent would be Daddy.

The first thirty years of His life are summed up in the affirmation from His Abba at the River Jordan when Jesus was baptized: **This is My beloved Son, in whom I am well-pleased** (Matthew 3:17). *Never once, in all the information we have concerning Jesus, did He try to earn His Father's love or even wonder whether He was loved; that was forever settled, an absolute He never questioned. He only* *chose to live in the consciousness of that love every hour of the day.*

We can never understand His joy, peace, command of every situation, teachings, or miracles apart from this one fact. This is the canvas upon which everything Jesus said and did is painted. Jesus lived in the knowledge that He was loved; He rose in the morning to it, went through the day in the confidence of it, and lay down to sleep knowing that He and all His tomorrows were in His Abba's hands.

Life With People

Jesus loved His fellow man as humans were originally intended to love, out of an inner fullness...not out of a need to evoke love from another person. God's love is not driven or compulsive, and love which is driven, a love born of need, does not have its origin in God. God freely *chose* to love us; He did not *need* us to complete something lacking in Himself. Grace, by definition, is that free choice on God's part to love the undeserving.

Jesus responded to His Father's love by listening to His inner voice and giving instant obedience to His every direction. He taught the people and healed the sick because of the pressing urgency of His Father's love; when He saw the multitudes, He was moved with compassion. But in implementing that love, He followed His Father's lead rather than

23

the multitude of people who mobbed Him, each demanding that He meet their needs first. *He was first committed to obeying the Father, and the people who clamored for His attention took second place.*

The Jesus we meet in the Gospels is not fretfully trying to meet everyone's needs so they will love Him and affirm Him as Messiah. He knows He is infinitely loved by His Father, and so, He does not come to the multitudes who press Him on every side with their needs with a compulsion to be loved. Rather, He comes to them having listened to the Father, knowing what His Father wants for the people, knowing what is required of Him to do, and doing it—no more and no less. His love service to His fellow man originates in His love service of listening to His Father. Doing the Father's work, He always drew on the power of the Holy Spirit to accomplish it.

It may be shocking to you, but Jesus did not go through life compulsively needing the love and acceptance of every human being. He could never have told them the truth if that had been the case, for He would have needed them too much! We must face the fact that, most of the time, when people were offended by Him, it was because He didn't fit in with their agenda!

Jesus, the perfect man, only had a few people we would put into the category of human friends. John was probably the best friend Jesus had, along with Peter and James. Mary, Martha, and Lazarus were a family of close friends with whom He could relax away from the crowds. When God visited earth and became a true human, He only had about six close friends! The rest either did not understand what He said or did, and were upset with Him, or they hated Him and tried to kill Him!

Emotional Reality

Humility, which is the key to peace of mind in the world, is simply living in reality, coming to terms with the way things really are. It is fully knowing our humanness and living comfortably in it. This means knowing our limitations, as well as our areas of ability, and offering all to God for His use as He lives unlimited in us. It also means recognizing that others have abilities which we do not have and letting them serve us with them.

Jesus lived in the reality of His humanness and knew what the Father wanted to accomplish through Him. He never sinfully fretted that He could not do more. He was fully aware that He couldn't be what the people of Israel wanted Him to be. In fact, He was the greatest of disappointments to the Jewish people, and He knew it. They had an image of their Messiah that didn't fit reality, so they wanted Jesus to be more than He was and to give more than He could give. If He had listened to them and, out of need for their approval, tried to be all that they wanted, He would have been less than Messiah! He would have sinned and certainly not been the Savior of God's specifications. He knew the people to whom He was sent were disappointed in Him, yet He lived in perfect peace, knowing He was completely fulfilling the Father's job description for His life.

The people of Nazareth could not handle His claims to fulfill Old Testament prophecies and would have killed Him if they could have (Luke 4:28-30). As a true human, Jesus would have deep emotional hurt knowing that the boys He went to school with now wanted Him dead. But He chose to live in the reality of their inability to see God's Messiah in the familiar face of their next-door neighbor. He moved the center of His operations to Capernaum and strengthened Himself with the words, **A prophet is not without honor except in his home town...** (Matthew 13:57).

He was surely a disappointment to the sick in Jerusalem when He was in Galilee. Living in the reality of His humanness, He knew that he could not be everywhere and heal everyone at the same time. You can be sure someone felt that the real Messiah ought to be omnipresent to heal them now! But He was limited, a true man, and could not be in all places at once. He never felt condemned that He had to leave people with their great needs and go on to the next place; He was directed by the Father, not by the needs of the people (Mark 1:35-38).

Jesus certainly upset Salome when He did not enthusiastically embrace her agenda for her two sons, James and John, to be seated next to Him in His kingdom (Matthew 20:20-28)! She wanted more from Him than He could give her. If Jesus had had a compulsive need for her to love and affirm Him, He would either have yielded to her or been thrown into a state of depression because He had offended an important supporter.

His close friends, Martha and Mary, were disappointed in Him because He didn't heal Lazarus the way they expected Him to (John 11:21,32). And the mourners in Jairus' house wanted Him to be the consoler instead of the resurrector! They could not understand why He upset the funeral by raising Jairus' daughter from the dead (Matthew 9:23-25).

Even the disciples, who were with Him so much of the time, did not understand Him. He was never what they thought He should be, because He was working from another agenda. The disciples wanted Him to be there for them more than the Father allowed, and so, in a real sense, He was never enough for them; they wanted Him to understand their needs and fulfill their agenda.

27

When their boat was sinking on the Sea of Galilee, they awakened Jesus and tried to lay guilt on Him, that He had not been caring for them enough: **Teacher, do You not care that we are perishing?** (Mark 4:38). They meant, "You should not be sleeping! You should be here for us!" He was not enough for them. Jesus refused to take the guilt they tried to heap on Him, and quietly told them that they should grow up and use their own faith! They did not want to be responsible for their own lives, but desired to be looked after (Mark 4:37-41).

The disciples wanted Him to be a more militant Messiah, as did the people who tried to make Him king by force. They wanted Him to destroy the enemies of the Jewish people and tried to pressure Him into acting according to their racist thinking of what Messiah should be like. But Jesus would not be pressured and simply responded, **You do not know what kind of spirit you are of...**(Luke 9:53-55).

It is important for us not to overlook the fact that Jesus knew He was a great disappointment to the twelve. But He also knew that He had expressed the Father's love to them, and He slept at night without anxiety for having hurt and confused His closest lieutenants.

Peter, along with the others, was disappointed that He spoke of suffering and death on a cross. Obviously, a suffering Messiah was not going to be the One of power and earthly glory of Whom they had always dreamed. They were further offended when He responded to Peter's words of concern and worldly-wise advice with the rebuke, **Get behind Me Satan.**..(Matthew 16:21-23).

Emotional Freedom

Because He was directed by His Father and not the demands of the people, Jesus had balance in His life and was able to take time to be alone with a few close friends without any sense of guilt. He could sleep during the daytime because He was tired, and be awakened to an emergency to calmly do what the Father wanted in the situation.

Living in the consciousness of being loved directed the way Jesus conducted Himself with other human beings. He was never anxious or fretful as to whether He had met the expectations of the people. Success in life for Him was in responding to the Father's love and doing what He wanted Him to do. To Him that was enough, and He rested with joy and peace that He had done all that was required.

His love for people must be understood as primarily responding in obedience to the Father's love, not in trying to meet all of the people's needs. He was totally dependent on the Father, listening only to Him and doing what He was told, however insignificant it seemed. In this relationship, He was the totally-fulfilled human being, therefore bringing glory to His Father.

Talking to an insignificant moral outcast in Samaria because His Father wanted Him to brought Him great joy (John 4:4-34), and there are many other examples of Jesus' sensitive response to God's direction in His ministry. However, the last twenty-four hours Jesus spent on earth in the company of His disciples show what the God kind of love expressed in ministry is really like.

After three years of public and private teaching, the disciples were going to the Upper Room to eat the Last Supper. They were angrily comparing themselves to each other, arguing as to who was the greatest, their eyes fixed on positions in the physical kingdom they still believed Jesus was going to set up in Jerusalem. The division was present even in Peter, James, and John, who prepared the dinner. Lest they should be perceived as less than the others, all three refused to accept the lowliest position in a Jewish household, that of the the one whose duty was to wash the feet of the other guests as they arrived.

How does Jesus react? If He had operated from the toxic, counterfeit form of love, He would have had thoughts like, "They are very upset tonight; it must be My fault! If I had been all they needed Me to be, they would be smiling and happy. I will have to take responsibility and do the job Myself." Or, "After three years of teaching them true greatness, they are arguing like this. I am a total failure." Or, "I can't stand arguing tonight—not tonight! Everything has to be just right and perfect on a night like this. I will wash their feet, and maybe that will make them happy."

Instead, the Scripture takes time to tell us exactly what Jesus' attitude was:

...Jesus knowing that His hour had come that He should depart out of this world to the Father, having loved His own who were in the world, He loved them to the end...knowing that the Father had given all things into His hands, and that He had come forth from God, and was going back to God, rose from supper, and laid aside His garments; and taking a towel, He girded Himself about.

John 13:1-4

Jesus loved and served out of the fullness of knowing the love the Father had for Him. Knowing His eternal worth, He did not do what He did in order to give Himself a sense of well-being or significance, or to make Himself lovable to the disciples. He acted out of Who He knew Himself to be.

True Love Brings Divine Wisdom

Observe how Jesus dealt with the problem person in the group. Peter was known for his mindless prattle and the ability to say the wrong thing at the wrong time. Now he is boasting of how he will never forsake Jesus, and at the same time, he is cruelly accusing everyone else of leaving Him in His time of need.

The Spirit revealed to Jesus that Satan would sift Peter like wheat on the threshing floor, and in that spiritual nightmare, Peter would deny he ever knew Jesus. Knowing that Jesus loves Peter, at this crisis moment, how does real Love express Himself?

Jesus saw the others as being infinitely loved by His Father and having to make their own choices about that love, choices He could not and would not make for them. When the real Messiah turns up among us, He does not interfere with anyone's life by protecting them from their own decisions! Only false, toxic messiahs do that. Jesus supported them with counsel He received from His Abba and also with prayer—but not by trying to make their decisions for them or by protecting them from the results of their choices.

If His love had been a toxic counterfeit, He might have said, "Peter, it's been a long day; I want you to stay home tonight. There might be some trouble later on, and I think you would be better off getting a good night's sleep!" He would have fixed Peter's problem by taking the responsibility to shield Peter from himself.

Or, He might have prayed: "Father, don't let this happen to Peter. We have kept his big mouth out of the press, and you know he doesn't mean half of what he says. His problem is our family secret. He means well, and we don't want to embarrass him and all of us with him, do we?" Toxic lovers forever make excuses and seek to cover for the person from whom they seek approval.

Nor does He tell Peter that He will make it all right, and that after the denial, he can just go home to bed and Jesus will make a few phone calls and cover for him, paying John off to keep him from telling the rest of the disciples. Furthermore, Jesus did not tell Peter that he was not responsible because his fearfulness was an inherited weakness in his genes! Foolish! But false, toxic love will go to any lengths to shield the person it seeks to help from the pain of facing their responsibility as a person made in God's image. *This counterfeit love has one goal, and that is to make the other person feel happy, for it is in their smile that it finds its own happiness.*

For Jesus, however, loving the one who was about to deny Him meant a number of things. First,

He assured Peter that He would *pray* for him, giving him the support he really needed. Jesus gave him encouragement that there was *hope* after the sin was over and dealt with. Then He left Peter to *grow up* by being forced to see himself and make his own decisions, as a responsible adult in the light of the Father's love (Luke 22:31-34).

When Peter fell, Jesus did not reject him or heap condemnation or say, "I told you so." Rather, He was there to move him into a new life of responsible loving (John 21:15-17).

Chapter Four

A GODLY SENSE OF SELF

Jesus died for His enemies—for all of us. He did not love His neighbor *as* Himself, but *more than* Himself, in choosing to die for us. But doesn't that sound similar to some of those we have described, who operate out of a false and sinful imitation of divine love?

We must remember the godly principle of Christian action we have established: Jesus was not seeking to do His works in order to be loved, either by the Father or by those to whom He ministered. The love of the Father was so real and totally satisfying to Him, that how others looked at Him and treated Him was second to that all-fulfilling relationship with the Father. *There was no inner, unsatisfied need in Jesus that made Him die for us so that we would love Him.*

Under Command

Jesus died for us, His enemies, not because He hoped that in so doing He would gain our love, but because the Father commanded Him to do so. In that sense, the death of Jesus was the crown of His life, because all His life He had done only what the Father willed. In the Garden of Gethsemane, He uttered the words which controlled His life, **...not My will, but Thine be done** (Luke 22:42).

Jesus was a true person, a true self, the blueprint of man that God intended us all to be. *A true self does not look after the self, but chooses to surrender it to God, to listen to and obey Him.* This is the life of joy, peace, meaning, and significance; at the same time, it is often the life of self-sacrifice, even to death.

If Jesus had died to help people, it would have been pointless, a wasted heap of ashes; but, because He died at the Father's command, He was exalted to be their Savior and Rescuer. Likewise, Christians are called to obey God, not to go around laying down their lives for everyone who asks them to, ending up on the ash heap and whimpering that no one cares.

Whenever we are simply responding to people's needs out of our own deep need for love, we are always disappointed, for very few of those we try to help will care enough to even say thank you! But if we act because the Father commands us to, then we know that we are part of a greater whole, and our sacrifice is knitted into the ongoing purpose of God.

Christians lay down their lives for the people their Abba tells them to! And so, in it all, they have the strengthening of the Holy Spirit, they have a joy set before them, and they know they are not alone.

Joy Unspeakable

Again, it was in West Africa that I sat in a hut. The walls were made of mud strengthened with tree branches, and the roof was made of many layers of grass woven through branches. A hole in the roof let out the smoke from the fire that burned in the middle of the floor. In the corner was a narrow bed, and a cuckoo clock hung on the mud wall.

Opposite me, in an ancient rocking chair, sat a charming American lady, old enough to be my grandmother, knitting a sweater. I had come on behalf of the churches that supported her, to plead with her to come home to a well-earned retirement. At seventy-five years old, she had served the people of this tribe for forty years. She smiled and told me to cash in the ticket, which I had brought with me for her trip home to Michigan.

She had laid down her life for these people—but it was not a heap of ashes. It was the expression of the love of God in and through her. She had obeyed God her Father, which involved laying down her life in the power of the Spirit for these people for these many years. Dying to her own will, she lived in the resurrection of joy and peace, and that mud hut was a palace to her. In fact, I felt I was sitting in the presence of royalty!

I have seen pastors and lay leaders lay down their lives for their flocks, and do so at the Father's command, with the result that they have vibrant mental and emotional health. These Christians find fulfillment in loving others with sacrificial love.

Jesus taught that we would be filled with a joy unspeakable when we fulfilled the reason for our being by loving one another with God's love. In Luke 15, in three parables, He tells of the neighbors and friends gathering to celebrate the finding of the lost; in one of these parables, the return of the prodigal son resulted in killing the fatted calf and dancing and rejoicing.

But take careful note: The shepherd didn't go looking for the sheep in order to have a celebration where he would be honored for his heroic rescue! Nor did the father welcome home the rebel son because he desperately needed to eat the calf and have an all-night party. If that had been the case, he would have regularly scoured the neighborhood, looking for anyone who was lost and even remotely connected to his family so that he could kill another calf.

The overflowing joy that comes when God's love in us acts is the *bonus* that is thrown in, not the *reason* for the act. We act upon His guidance and direction because of our deep love for Him, which emanates from the unconditional love He has shown us. And the result of our love action is that we are miraculously filled with and surrounded by His unspeakable joy.

Chapter Five

LIVING IN HIS LOVE

As you have been reading, have you seen yourself as a person who has been operating out of a toxic love base? Some of you are letting **the worry of the world** that Jesus spoke of choke off the life of God which is in you (Matthew 13:22). Find victory here and Satan will have lost an effective entrance to your life!

If God has spoken to you through these words, then do not put off acting on what He has said. I suggest that you reread those portions of this book which especially apply to you and own any trace of toxic love in your life as your personal sin before God. Call it what it is—idolatry—putting the creature in the place of the Creator. It is looking for your identity and meaning in life in another human being's bestowal of love and acceptance instead of the Father's.

As you read through this book again, ask the Holy Spirit, your resident Counselor, to show you any areas where you may be blind. Remember that repentance is a change of mind, and it is just such a total turnaround of thinking concerning the true nature of love that the Holy Spirit is achieving in you as you read.

He has shown you the nature of real love and the idolatry of counterfeit, toxic love. Upon identifying your attitudes and ways of relating to people that are a work of the flesh, independent of God, renounce them and put them away from you. When Jesus died, He put to death rebellious flesh (Romans 6:6). We can do nothing to bring sin to an end in our lives except to thank God that, in Jesus Christ, He has brought it to death so that He may live His life in us.

Next, having seen the sin of false love and repenting of it, how do we love as believers? How do we love, **...as I have loved you**? Perhaps the answers are in the following letter, which I wrote to someone who, having heard me teach on toxic love, asked those questions.

Dear Sally,

I praise God with you that you have seen the emptiness and spiritual death in the way you have been relating to others. Now begins the real business of living your daily lifestyle in the love that the

New Testament speaks of: the life for which you were created that is found in Jesus Christ.

We love others with the love which comes from God—not by trying, but by realizing that we ourselves are loved. We have seen that we were created to receive and live in union with the God who loves us unconditionally. Jesus, the sinless, normal man, awoke to the consciousness of that love in His childhood years.

But what about mankind? As unbelievers, we are separated from God, believing the Lie that we can have a fulfilling life apart from God, and rebelliously trying to prove it true in our lives. It is right here that the unconditional love of God is seen in its vastness.

Love is a Gift

In Jesus Christ, the God we have sinned against took to Himself our humanity and entered our race. He took to Himself our sin and our determination to be our own god; He also took the pain and grief that we had brought upon ourselves through our willful rebellion. He then bore the punishment of our sin and died as us and for us, carrying the entire rebellion into the grave, and rising again as the Source of the real life and love that we had rejected.

The living Jesus is the final word of God saying to us, "I love you." The great secret of spiritual, mental, and emotional health is summed up in the words, **We love, because He first loved us** (First John 4:19).

As Jesus lived in the consciousness of His Father's unlimited love, so it is with us. In our inner selves we live in the consciousness of His love, which gives us life in the same way our physical bodies live in air and fish live in the sea.

When Paul prayed for the early believers to live in the freedom of truly loving one another, he begins by praying that they might come to **...know the love of Christ which surpasses knowledge...** (Ephesians 3:19). Only after that prayer did he call them, in Chapters 4 and 5, to live out the love of God in their daily relationships. And the life to which he exhorted them is supernatural! **...Forgiving each other, just as God in Christ also has forgiven you...and walk in love, just as Christ also loved you...**(Ephesians 4:32, 5:2).

The fact that he did not instruct them, but *prayed* that they would see God's love, would indicate that the knowledge or experience of it must be given by God. It cannot be studied out, nor is it merely a worked-up feeling; it is the gift of God— but a gift that is easy to receive. By giving us this prayer in Ephesians 3:19, the Holy Spirit authorizes us to ask and to expect the gift of supernatural love to be ours.

The gift of unconditional love comes to us in the form of the power—or ability—of the Holy Spirit. **...the love of God is shed abroad in our hearts by the Holy Ghost which is given to us** (Romans 5:5). *The Holy Spirit actually enables us, gives us the wisdom, and strengthens our wills so that we become the love of God to those around us.*

Paul, praying for this love to be received by the Colossians, again referred to its source being in the power of the Holy Spirit: **...strengthened with all power, according to His glorious might, for the attaining of all steadfastness and patience...** (Colossians 1:11).

Both the words **strengthened** and **power** are defined in Acts 1:8 as the power which comes from the Holy Spirit. **Patience** is the love of God in us, exercised toward the most unlovable of persons.

This God kind of love "surpasses," or goes far beyond, all human knowledge (Ephesians 3:19). We are dealing with the nature of the infinite God being experienced in the life of finite man. There is no limit to the experience and no end to such an adventure!

Because of this, the early Christians continually prayed that they would know the constant flow of supernatural love into their lives:

Paul prayed for the Philippians, **And this I pray, that your love may abound still more and more**

in real knowledge and all discernment (Philippians 1:9).

For the Thessalonians he prayed, **...may the Lord cause you to increase and abound in love for one another, and for all men** (First Thessalonians 3:12).

Receiving the Gift of Love

In order to let such prayers be answered, I suggest that you set aside time every day to sit in God's presence, not to pray to or perform something for Him, but *just to be loved by Him.* Begin by praying these prayers, and then sit and be aware of the Father God Who loves you, Who has come to you through Jesus Christ and now fills you by His Spirit. Let the reality that you have been personally loved by God as He foreknew you in innumerable ages past, and as He dwells within you at this moment, flood your whole person. You can say, **[He] loved me, and delivered Himself up for me** (Galatians 2:20b).

You discover who you are in this very real inter-action with God, your Creator, Who, through Jesus Christ, is your Father. *Here is where you admit you are primarily a spirit person who cannot function without knowing you are infinitely and uncondi-tionally loved.* And, I might add, although it is not the prime reason for spending time with Him, it is in this stillness and in the consciousness of being loved that you learn to listen to what God is saying to you.

These times of opening yourself to God's love are equivalent to the priority time that Jesus gave to being alone with His Father, both in the early morning and late at night. The place and amount of time given to this are not important. It is the opening of our innermost self to God that counts.

I know an executive in Manhattan with an impossible schedule, who stops on the hour every hour for a couple of minutes to realize he is a child of God, infinitely and unconditionally loved. He does the same thing in the middle of hectic days, when work threatens to dehumanize him.

There is a housewife in Tulsa who takes twenty minutes in the morning after the children have gone to school and twenty minutes in the evening before going to bed to let the love of God soak into her inner being. And a high school student takes ten minutes of his lunch break to sit in the living Presence and know the meaning of life—being loved by the Creator.

Expressing the Gift of Love

How do we take the love that we receive from the Holy Spirit and live it in a dog-eat-dog world? How do we love like Jesus? The only answer to that question is, *only Jesus can love like Jesus!*

Christianity does not claim to be a philosophy of life, but to be Life Himself living within us. In that sense, there is no such thing as Christian morality in terms of a list of do's and don'ts, but rather, the spontaneous living of Christ Himself through our lives. In this day of formulas and the packaged "how-to-do-it" seminars, Christianity is the odd man out, for the Gospel calls us to commit not to a formula, but to a Person Who is, Himself, the Way. When Christianity has become a philosophy or a formula, it falls apart and becomes a list of impossible ideals.

But Christianity is not *idealistic*. It is preeminently *realistic,* for it is founded on the fact that Jesus Christ is alive from the dead and is now communicating His life to us by the Holy Spirit! And His life is, of course, the love that we are talking about.

We do not move from toxic love to the love of Jesus by getting a new grip on ourselves, nor by making a decision to be selfish and look after ourselves, but by giving ourselves to the Lord Jesus Christ. Surrendering to Jesus is a radical change that begins a process in us, a process in which we learn to receive His communicated life under all of life's varied relationships and circumstances.

Having prayed and opened ourselves to the love of God, we begin to take steps of faith. To the Thessalonians, Paul wrote, **...you...are taught by**

**God to love one another...*you do practice
it...*we urge you, brethren, to excel still
more...**(First Thessalonians 4:9,10).

I suggest you do this, first of all, by taking every
relationship you are involved in, whether with
people, organizations, volunteer work, or commit-
tees, and laying them before the Lord. I usually do
this with pen and paper or sitting at the computer; I
find I can sort out what He is saying to me much
better if I can see it in front of me. Ask Him to turn
His light upon each relationship and show you anything you are doing that is originating in the flesh
and is a toxic, false love. Ask Him to tell you what
He wants you to do with and in the relationship. Let
your prayer always be, "Lord Jesus, live through me
in this relationship."

Daily Battles to be Won

Each morning, be aware that you must be on
your guard or you can very quickly be pulled back
into the old paths. You are involved in a war! **For
the flesh sets its desire against the Spirit, and
the Spirit against the flesh; for these are in
opposition to one another...**(Galatians 5:17).

When you see a need, you will probably feel the
pull of the flesh to handle it as you always have in
the past, as if you are responsible to fill it. There will
also be an army of people you have unwittingly

drawn towards you who expect you to be their refuge, strength, and the messiah who is always there for them.

As they come once more into the orbit of your life, this time it may be well to share with them a testimony of what God has done with you and then make it a matter of prayer as to what, if any, involvement you are going to have with them.

There is another subtle temptation you should be aware of: People are going to share their needs with you today, not because they want you to get involved, but because they want someone to talk to! Do not run their needs through your flesh computer, which will distort God's will for you and interpret their sharing as asking you to help. Offer your ears to Jesus so that He may teach you to listen and pass all the information on to Him in prayer with no compulsion to get involved.

Remember, Sally, you now live from the solid base that *you are not a self-pleaser, not a people-pleaser, nor a need-meeter, but a Father-pleaser in the power of the Holy Spirit.* You know the nature of the temptation now—the old inclination to find love and acceptance in people instead of in God. You choose not to respond with the inner words, "If I don't, who will?" "Well, I guess I should," or "OK, just this once...." No, this time you are making these things truly a matter of prayer, and you will not be pressured. Learn to live in submission to the Lord Jesus and not to needs and people. When all is said and done, the only way you can meet anyone's needs is by being submitted to *Him*.

You are no longer driven to become involved with every need or person who drifts across your path. Instead, you pray, "Father, I thank You that You are this person's refuge and strength and the perfect answer to their need. If You want to use me beyond my committing them to You now in prayer, I am available. If not, I leave them in Your hands and thank You that they are safe with You."

Now, don't go overboard—which the flesh loves to do! If you are being paid to do a job, you do not have to ask the Father whether you should do it! Rather, you should pray for the strength to give it your total attention and to do it to the best of your ability.

If, however, you are doing someone else's work, which they are paid to do, and neglecting yours, that situation needs the renovating power of the Spirit! And, if I know you, Sally, you probably have been the mother hen to everyone you work with, feeding their laziness and irresponsibility by doing their work and neglecting your own!

And don't start asking God if you are supposed to continue being married to Arthur! You have only one responsibility there, and that is to let the Holy

Spirit show you any area where toxic love is eating away at your marriage and to renounce it.

Seeing Through Jesus' Eyes

Communicating with the Father through Jesus Christ, Who is your life, may sound strange to some, but it is your truest sense of reality. For this you were made: to live in communication with your Father and live with His life. It is perfectly normal to live by His direction rather than by "ought's," "should's," or guilt feelings, all of which belong to the flesh. It is only in a world of abnormals that normalcy seems odd and different!

As you are freed from the bondages of toxic love, you will begin to look at people in a new way—through Jesus' eyes. You will see more clearly that God is at work in their lives, and for you to rush in and fix them to the specifications of your personal, biased blueprint will probably frustrate what God is about to do.

Remember how Jesus handled Peter. If He had rescued Peter from confronting his empty self, we would never have heard of the blustering fisherman. God allowed Satan limited access to Peter in order to bring him to a real death to all trust in himself—so that he might discover for himself the life of Jesus united with him.

As a little boy, I saw a butterfly struggling to free itself from its chrysalis. I took a razor blade and delicately cut him loose. But the poor creature never flew, and it died on the window seat. Later I discovered that the butterfly's wing muscles receive their strength for flight in the process of coming out of the chrysalis.

How many people have we "rescued" into utter weakness and spiritual death? Sally, you must learn that you are not God, and *your place in the lives of others is to bring them to Him and leave them with Him as you uphold them in prayer.*

You will know when you have fallen into the ways of the flesh in this area because all of the old disgust with yourself and people will be back, along with your frustration and self-hate. Do not plunge on like a runaway horse! And don't withdraw in despair calling yourself a failure. Just stop and receive forgiveness, then get out of whatever flesh involvement you are in.

Emotional freedom is not going to happen overnight! You are going to gradually grow into a continual realization of the love of God and a genuine love for people, accepting them as they are, and not as you think they should be; putting them into God's hands, and recognizing they are His project instead of making them yours!

There will be some people to whom you know the Father wants you to minister, and you will give yourself to God for the task and do it in the power of His Spirit. However, you must understand that this does not mean that the person will respond. If you are doing the work for them and for your own sense of identity and meaning, then such a response will make you mad at them and you will dismiss yourself as an abysmal failure. But if you have followed me so far, then you will see that *your success in life is in having done what the Father wanted you to do.* You are free to feel the longing of the Father's heart for the people, without expecting or relying upon anything from them in return.

Jesus spoke on the streets of Jerusalem, but they rejected Him. Finally, He stood on Olivet and wept with great sobs. It would seem to us that He had failed! But His sobs were not out of frustration or anger, but for the people who had turned down their only hope of salvation. He went on without any sense of being a failure, for He had done the Father's will.

In a sense, you are entering into the adventure of the Christian life for the first time, even though you have been born again for ten years! It is the adventure of letting Jesus live His life of divine love through you. Step out and start walking on the water—He will teach you!

In Christ Jesus, M.S.